JESUS IS THE ANSWER

JESUS
IS THE
ANSWER

PASTOR DR. DERICKLYN PARKER

XULON PRESS

Xulon Press
2301 Lucien Way #415
Maitland, FL 32751
407.339.4217
www.xulonpress.com

Unless otherwise indicated, Scripture quotations taken from the King James Version (KJV) – *public domain.*

Printed in the United States of America.

ISBN-13: 9781545676318

Table of Contents

———————※———————

Dedication

───────※───────

This book is dedicated to the Man
who left His throne in Heaven, came
to earth and gave His life for me,
Jesus Christ, my Lord and my Savior
who has been my Answer since the
age of twelve.
-Thank You Jesus-

Thank You

———————— ✳ ————————

A very special thank you to The Holy
Spirit of God who I depend on for
truth, for help, and for guidance.
-Thank you Holy Spirit-
A special Thank you to my spiritual
Mom, Pastor Ernestine Garries, for
all the love, much needed prayers,
review, editing and support of this
book. I appreciate you, Mom.
To my grandmother, my parents and
siblings, I love you.
Thank you to my beloved husband
James Parker for your countless support through the years. You are truly
a God sent just for me.
Thank you to Jalyn-Grace for showing
me how to have childlike Faith.

May 17th, 2019

Jesus is the Answer

———————✳———————

*B*ecause you are reading this booklet this may be your last chance to make Jesus Christ the Lord of your life! Your days of trying to do things on your own can be over IF you will make the decision to accept Jesus Christ into your heart today. Jesus Christ said He will never leave you neither will He for-sake you and you will spend eternity with Him forever, because NOW you are His.

Life itself is filled with surprises, some are welcomed and some are not. Nevertheless, the surprises you receive will not catch you off guard because Jesus Christ will be on your side.

Let me start by saying when you accept Jesus Christ into your heart and make Him Lord of your life does not mean that everything will be easy for you. But Jesus Christ is always alongside of you to help bear any burden and hardship that may arise.

Remember, because Jesus Christ loves you, He died for you, He promise to return to bring you to His Father. He will make good on all His promises that is written in the Scriptures from Genesis through Revelation, giving us the good life, both now and forever as we walk with Him and obey His commandants.

I must be very clear in this, Jesus Christ did not die because He wanted to, He died because He needed to in order to fulfill God's promise and intention for us to be with Him before the fall of Adam and Eve. He saw that we were all doomed and headed to a life in eternal hell and damnation, which is a place of torment, agony, pain and suffering. Those who make the decision to exclude Jesus Christ out of their life, hell is their place of final rest. Revelation 14:11, declared, "And the smoke of their torment ascendeth up for ever and ever: and they have no rest day nor night, who worship the beast and his image, and whosoever receiveth the mark of his name." This should not describe your fate.

There is no escaping hell for there is a great partition between heaven and hell so that those who are in heaven cannot cross over to hell to help anyone who made their decision to go there, and those in hell cannot get out and seek shelter. Furthermore, the Scriptures also declare, that the rich man in hell, lifted up his eyes being in torment and seeing Abraham a distance away, Lazarus the poor man being comforted in the bosom of Abraham, the rich man cried out and said Father Abraham, have mercy on me, and send Lazarus, that he may dip the tip of his finger in water, and cool my tongue; for I am tormented in this flame. But Abraham said, Son, remember that you in your lifetime received good things, and contrary, Lazarus received evil things: and now he is comforted, and you are tormented. Besides all this, there is a great partition between you and us: so that no one could pass from you to us and us to you. Then the rich man said, would you send Lazarus to my father's house because I have five brothers that he may testify unto them about SALVATION, lest they also come into this place of torment as I am. And Abraham said to the rich man, they have Moses and the Prophets; let them hear (listen) to them. And he said, No, father Abraham: but if someone went from the dead, they would believe and repent. And Abraham said to him, If they will not listen to Moses and the Prophets, nor will they be persuaded, to listen from anyone who has risen from the dead. (Reference, Luke 19)

It is said by many that "there is no God." The Bible clearly states in Genesis, "In the beginning God...." This Scripture held true for over 2000 years ago and is being fulfill today and full-proof that everything God has said, is true and still holds. (Reference Genesis 1:1). The question asked by some, "If there is a God, why does He allow bad things to happen?" In the Book of Ecclesiastes 3:1-8, "To every thing there is a season, and a time to every purpose under the heaven: A time to be born, and a time to die; a time to plant, and a time to pluck up that which is planted; A time to kill, and a time to heal; a time to break down, and a time to build up; A time to weep, and a time to laugh; a time to mourn, and a time to dance; A time to cast away stones, and a time to gather stones together; a time to embrace, and a time to refrain from embracing; A time to get, and a time to lose; a time to keep, and a time to cast away; A time to rend, and a time to sew; a time to keep silence, and a time to speak; A time to love, and a time to hate; a time of war, and a time of peace." Everything has a reason and sometimes it's beyond our comprehension, but God always knows what's best for His children.

I will say to you that nothing happens on the earth without God being aware. Sometimes He permits things to happen to draw us to Him and some-things He does not permit to happen because it could devastate us. When things happen in your life that make you question the reality of God's Sovereignty, it is important to have Him (God) on your side. Going through life without Jesus Christ has proven to be a disaster for many whose lives have been lost to damnation because they chose not to have Jesus Christ as their SAVIOR.

Jesus Christ made it abundantly clear through the Scriptures to all His beloved followers that in this world we will have tests, trials, tribulations, trou-bles, disappointments, oppressions and oppositions nevertheless; Jesus Christ tells us to, "BE OF GOOD CHEER," for He has overcome the world. (Reference, John 16:33). For Greater is He, Jesus

Christ that is in you than he (Satan), troubles etc., that is in the world. (Reference, 1John 4:4). So if God be for you, who can stand against you? It is better to go through life with Jesus Christ than to go through life without Him. Therefore, Jesus Christ offers you hope, why not accept it right now?

To present a picture of what Satan offers is: a life of pleasure, eye appealing luxury, free fun, easy money, sensual pleasure to the eyes and body that are all short live. These are temporal and damming, enabling you to get yourself into an all-consuming trap that you will not be able to get out of. Is that what you want?

The general consensus should be of everything that is right and holy to pre-serve mankind in the state that God has created for him to enjoy through Jesus Christ, is why God sent His only Son into the World. God loved us so much because we were doomed to a life of hell that He sacrificed His Son for us, to bring us back to where we belong in the very beginning before the world was spoken into existence. (Reference John 1:1).

Every moment of your life is watched from heaven and recorded in the books that God has whether you have accepted Jesus Christ as your personal Lord and Savior or you have chosen to walk without Him. Everything is accounted for whether it is good, bad or indifferent. You will be rewarded for it. Scripture says, you reap what you sow, Galatians 6:3-9, "For if a man think himself to be something, when he is nothing, he deceiveth himself. But let every man prove his own work, and then shall he have rejoicing in himself alone, and not in another. For every man shall bear his own burden. Let him that is taught in the word communicate unto him that teacheth in all good things. Be not deceived; God is not mocked: for whatsoever a man soweth, that shall he also reap. For he that soweth to his flesh shall of the flesh reap corruption; but he that soweth to the Spirit shall of the Spirit reap life everlasting. And let us not be weary in well doing: for in due season we shall reap, if we faint not."

Jesus Christ is waiting for you to callout to Him and ask Him to come into your life because of His love for you. He wants to show you what true love is. His love never fails, through the good times and the bad. His love grows greater for you each day. The Scripture tells us, Lamentations 3:22-23, "It is of the Lord's mercies that we are not consumed, because his compassions fail not. They are new every morning:

great is thy faithfulness." So this tells you that He is willing to bear whatever hardship you have and burdens you carry. For He is well equipped to do so if you trust Him and only lean on Him. He will work everything out for your good, Romans 8:28, "And we know that all things work together for good to them that love God, to them who are the called according to his purpose."

If you are wondering how do I talk to God? The answer is just speak to Him as you would a best friend, someone you have known for a very long time and close to. In Scripture, He says He is a friend that sticks closer than a brother, Proverb 18:24, "A man that hath friends must shew himself friendly: and there is a friend that sticketh closer than a brother." Tell Jesus about your feelings, who hurt you, the abandonment you felt, the fear, the anxiety, the depression, the insecurity, the love that was lost, the molestations that have happened, the beatings and rape and murders you may have witnessed and heard about that have affected you mentally physically and spiritually. God is able to heal all wounds, remove all fear and indelible impressions, and renew a right spirit in you. He will give you a clean heart and erase all memories of agony and pain that have plagued you down through the years if you only give all to Him. (Reference Matthew 11:28-30). In other words, God is in the total renovation business. Jesus is The Answer!!!

May 17th, 2019

Try Jesus

———————✳———————

Are you searching for a life of purpose, a life of satisfaction, a life worth living, and a sense of fulfillment, but you have come away empty? You have tried everything including, sex, drugs, alcohol, and a fast pace life, spiraling downward and going nowhere. The friends you have made, you have now found out that they are not loyal nor can you depend on them for anything of value. And now you are at a place in your life where you are re-evaluating the importance of your existence. I ask you why not try Jesus Christ today? When all else fail, Jesus Christ will never fail you.

The world is filled with its methods and theories of how things ought to go and how things should work. However, what you have tried does not fit your personality and general make up. Why not try Jesus Christ. But Scripture tells us, Proverbs 3:5, "Trust in the Lord with all your heart and lean not to your own understanding, but in all your ways acknowledge God and He will direct your path." When you try Jesus Christ and follow His command-ments, one thing is certain, we do not need a plan A, B, C or D, all we need is Jesus Christ. He works everything out on time. The Scriptures are our roadmap to life's successes and our heart's satisfaction. Prosperity comes along with this, because His Word tells us so. Jeremiah 29:11-14, "For I know the thoughts that I think toward you, saith the LORD, THOUGHTS OF PEACE, AND NOT OF EVIL, TO GIVE YOU AN EXPECTED END. Then shall ye call upon me, and ye shall go and pray unto me, and I will hearken unto you. And ye shall seek me, and find me, when ye shall search for me with all your heart. And I will be found of you, saith the Lord: and I will turn away your captivity, and I will gather you from all the nations, and from all the places whither I have driven you, saith the Lord; and I will bring you again into the place whence I caused you to be carried away captive."

With these precious promises, coming from the mouth of God, we cannot lose trying Jesus Christ. Your life does not end here. When you leave this earth, the question is, where will your soul spend eternity? Will it be hell fire, eternal damnation where there is no escape because it was your choice? Or will it be Heaven where Jesus Christ is, a life everlasting, free of sorrow, free of pain and any remembrance of a past accusing life? WHY NOT TRY JESUS CHRIST?

May 17th, 2019

Give Jesus A Chance

———— ✳ ————

We are created in the image of God and because of that, He has made us free spirits in that we can choose life's chances of which some are sure and many are not. Nevertheless, chances comes to all of us. Ecclesiastes 3:1-8, "To every thing there is a season, and a time to every purpose under the heaven: A time to be born, and a time to die; a time to plant, and a time to pluck up that which is planted; A time to kill, and a time to heal; a time to break down, and a time to build up; A time to weep, and a time to laugh; a time to mourn, and a time to dance; A time to cast away stones, and a time to gather stones together; a time to embrace, and a time to refrain from embracing; A time to get, and a time to lose; a time to keep, and a time to cast away; A time to rend, and a time to sew; a time to keep silence, and a time to speak; A time to love, and a time to hate; a time of war, and a time of peace."

How many chances have you taken in life up to this point? Can you count them on one hand or both hands to include counting all your toes? Every day of your life you take chances. From the moment you wake up to the moment you go back to bed. You take a chance when your feet touch the floor in the morning that you will be able to stand. You take a chance when you brush your teeth hoping your gums won't bleed. You take a chance getting dressed making sure your zipper does not catch. You take a chance when you put your child or children on the school bus hoping that they are not injured in a collision and return home safely. You take a chance when you get behind the wheel of your car that your engine starts and drive on the road safely. You take a chance when you sit on a chair, no thought of whether it will support your weight or not. You take a chance when you enter a building hoping the beam does not collapse. You take a chance when you go out to eat that you don't develop an allergic reaction or get food poisoning and/or choke on your meal. You take a chance when you go on a blind date or with someone you know that will keep you safe. You take a chance when you stand at the altar of a church or courthouse and say, I do to the very one you entrust the rest of your life with that you will not be disappointed. You take a chance when you are expecting a child that the delivery will be safe and that the child will be healthy, whole and normal. And the list goes on.

More importantly, in these days and times, when a teacher enters the classroom with students that they are to teach, or when a lawyer enters the courtroom to defend a life that is holding between two foundations, or when parishioners enter their place of worship coming together in the spirit of love, peace and harmony and finally when a military person enters a contract with the government to uphold its constitution, to fight for the defense of his or her country, and upon entering foreign soil, not knowing if they will ever return to a place that they call home or a place of refuge, of all four of the above mentioned CHANCES ARE TAKEN.

So why not take a chance on a sure thing, someone who is able to keep you from falling, Jesus Christ, our Lord. This same Jesus Christ who presents Himself as your Lord and Savior was made to be the sacrificial lamb who died on the cross at Calvary, for every-thing that you would need a chance for. He is able to keep you, preserve you, sustain you, and last of all present you to His Father whereby you would become joint heirs with Him in the final days of eternity. It's very easy to see that he took a chance on you when He (Jesus Christ) offered Himself on that faithful day, because He needed to ful-fill His Father's plan to bring you back to Himself who is your Creator before the world existed. In other words, you belong to God before the fall of Adam and Eve ever happened. Therefore, God is just reclaiming you through the death, burial and the resurrection of his Son Jesus Christ. Jesus paid the price in full with His life taken, blood shed for all you could ever go through in your lifetime that you may come out whole, renewed, reborn and reclaimed by God Almighty.

I ask, how is your soul positioned? Is it aligned right with God? If you die this very moment, can you tell me where your soul will rest? The Bible says, in Matthew 5:8, "Blessed are the pure in heart: for they shall see God." In Revelation 21:4-8, "And God shall wipe away all tears from their eyes; and there shall be no more death, neither sorrow, nor crying, neither shall there be any more pain: for the former things are passed away. And he that sat upon the throne said, Behold, I make all things new. And he said unto me, Write: for these words are true and faithful. And he said unto me, It is done. I am Alpha and Omega, the beginning and the end. I will give unto him that is athirst of the fountain of the water of life freely. He that overcometh shall inherit all things; and I will be his God, and he shall be my son. But the fearful, and unbelieving, and the abominable, and murderers, and whoremongers, and sorcerers, and idolaters, and all liars, shall have their part in the lake which burneth with fire and brimstone: which is the second death."

God promises you that He would wipe away all tears from your eyes that He will be there whenever you need Him. He wanted these words to be written so that you clearly under-stand what awaits you if you choose not to give Jesus Christ a chance.

Remember verse 8 of Revelation says, "But the fearful and unbelieving and the abominable and the murderous and whoremongers and sorcerers and adulterers and all liars shall have their part in the lake which burneth with fire and brimstone, which is your second death." There is no return from this last life. Why not give Jesus Christ a chance? You have absolutely nothing to lose, but eternal life to gain.

If you have decided after reading this booklet that Jesus is the Answer to all your problems, and you would like to try Jesus Christ, make Him the Lord of your life, and give Jesus Christ a chance to show you what life will be like having Him reign and rule, guide and love you the way it should have been before all that you have gone through without Him, than do so right now because He, Jesus Christ is your Answer.

Please pray this prayer: God in Heaven, I believe that you sent your only Son Jesus Christ to die for me on the cross at Calvary to shed His Blood that cleanses me of all my sins, my sicknesses, my diseases and all my problems that I will ever face. I repent of all sins, all wrongdoings those that I know of and those don't know of. I ask forgiveness and invite you Jesus into my life to be Lord and Savior right now. I believe what you have done for me that all my sins are forgiven, they are washed away and remembered no more. (Reference Psalms 103:12). I am starting a new life with you Jesus from this day forward and I will never go back to the way I used to live. I choose to put my past behind me and the Cross of Salvation and all the ways the commandments teaches before me. My future is great because the Greater

One (Jesus Christ) lives inside of me. I will no longer be a slave yielding to sin. I no longer serve the devil, I am no longer bound in the chains of bondage but I am FREE. I am now a child of the King, I praise God for saving me.

Now that you have prayed the above Prayer, it is our pleasure as your sister and brother to welcome you into the family of God and joint heirs with Jesus Christ, our Lord. Because old things are passed away and you are now a brand new creature in Christ Jesus. 2 Corinthians 5:17, "Therefore if any man be in Christ, he is a new creature: old things are passed away; behold, all things are become new."

What do you do from here? The answer is read the Bible, suggestions King James, the Amplified, the New International Version, the Message, and New Living Translation. You may start with The Book of Psalms, Genesis, Exodus, Joshua, Jeremiah, Isaiah, Ezekiel, Matthew, Mark, Luke, John, Romans, The Acts of the Apostles and Revelation to name a few. Servitude: Whatever you are good at doing, begin to use your skills and talents to bring God glory. Find a good Bible believing church where you can be with true believers to strengthen each other as they walk with God and His statues. Thirdly, make Prayer a regular diet in your daily walk. In order to have good success, the Bible says in Joshua 1:8, to keep the Law (The Word) of God ever before you and meditate on it day and night.

I pray that you shall receive the Grace of God and prosper in everything you set your hands to do according to His perfect Will for you-AMEN.

For more information about the author and the works of Jesus Christ and greater works, please visit www.vesselofhonorministries.org

CPSIA information can be obtained
at www.ICGtesting.com
Printed in the USA
LVHW111410231219
641450LV00009BA/143/P

9 781545 676318